This is the story of Hapu. He lives in Ancient Egypt at the time of Queen Cleopatra.

His father, Bak, has a small factory. He makes gold tables and chairs. Hapu helps him. He is a 'fireboy'. Every day he pushes a long handle up and down. The work is hot and very hard. But what can he and his father do? They are poor people. They need to make money.

Every evening they sit beside the Nile. Bak talks to his
son about the factory, tomorrow's work – everything.
"One day we're going to be very rich," he tells Hapu.
"Are we?" The fireboy looks into his father's tired eyes.
"Yes." Bak smiles. "I don't know how and I don't know
when, but we are." Then he stands up. "Come on," he
says. "It's late. Let's go home."

Three days later Hapu and Bak are making a table. It is
very hot in the room. Suddenly Bak stops work.

"What is it, father?" Hapu asks. "Is something wrong?"

"I don't know," Bak answers. He closes his eyes.

"It's my head. I can't . . ." And then he falls on the ground.

"Father!" Hapu runs to Bak and puts one hand under
his head. "Father – are you all right?"

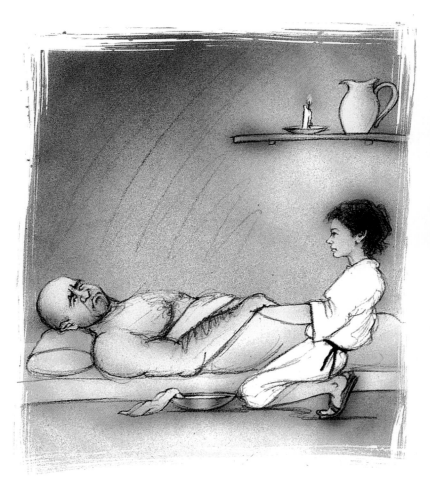

The next day Bak stays in bed. "I'm sorry Hapu," he
says. "I want to work but I can't. I'm ill."
Hapu is very sad. "Father works too hard," he thinks.
"That's why he's ill. We need more money – but what
can I do?" Then he has an idea. "Of course!" he thinks.
"I must make something for somebody very rich.
Somebody like . . . the Queen!"

Bak is ill for two weeks. In that time Hapu makes a lot of tables and chairs. But not only tables and chairs. He makes a gold necklace, too.

"There!" he thinks late one night. "It's ready." He smiles. The necklace is very beautiful. "Queen Cleopatra is going to like this," Hapu thinks. "She's going to pay a lot of money for it, too. I know she is."

The next morning he goes to Cleopatra's palace. The
necklace is in a bag under his shirt.

"What do *you* want?" asks a palace guard. There are
two guards. Each one has a sword.

"I want to see the Queen," Hapu answers.

Both guards laugh. "Go home, boy," says one of them.
"Queen Cleopatra doesn't see people like you."

Hapu is very unhappy. "What do I do now?" he thinks.
He leaves the palace and begins to walk home.
But ten minutes later he passes two men in the market.
"Cleopatra's women are coming here tomorrow
morning," says one. "They're arriving very early. They
want to buy lots of new clothes for her."
"That's very good news," Hapu thinks.

The next day the fireboy gets up very early. He makes a
cup of sweet tea for Bak. Then he goes to the market. "I
can give the necklace to Cleopatra's women," he thinks.
"They can give it to the Queen for me."

He waits and waits. For a long time nothing happens.
Then music starts to play. A moment later Hapu sees a
long line of people. They are coming from the palace.

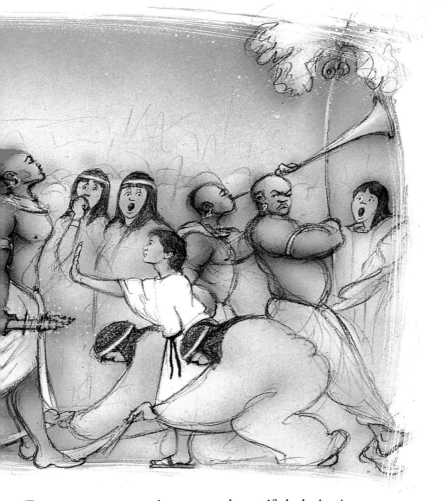

Four men are carrying a very beautiful chair. A woman
is sitting in it. Hapu puts one hand across his eyes. "It's
the Queen!" he thinks. "She's coming, too!"
A minute later Cleopatra arrives. Suddenly everyone is
very quiet. Then Hapu thinks, "This is the moment." He
runs in front of Cleopatra's chair. "Stop!" he says.
"*Please*. Stop!"

The Queen looks at him. "What do you want?" she
asks. Hapu gives her the necklace.

"Is this really *your* work?" asks Cleopatra.

"Yes, yes it is," Hapu answers.

"Guards!" says Cleopatra. "Give this boy some
money." She holds the necklace in her hands. "This is
beautiful," she says. Then she leaves.

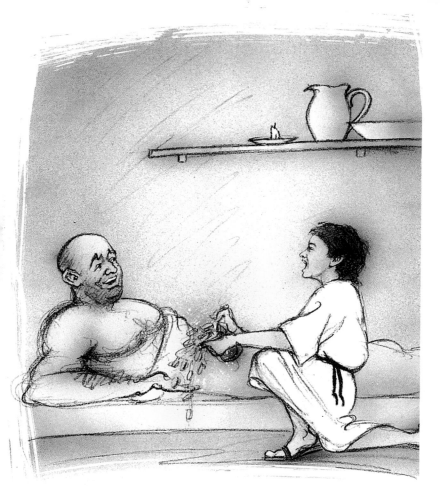

Hapu runs home. He is very, *very* happy.

Bak is in bed. "Look!" Hapu says. He shows the money from Cleopatra's necklace to his father.

"But how . . . ?" Bak closes his eyes, then opens them again. "I don't understand," he says. Hapu smiles. He sits down and tells his father everything. At the end of the story Bak says, "You're a good son, Hapu. Thank you."

That night Hapu looks up at the stars. "Now I can pay for a doctor to visit father," he thinks. "Then, after father is strong again . . ."

But at that moment he stops. One of Cleopatra's guards is standing in front of him. He has a big sword. "Are you Hapu, son of Bak?" he asks. Hapu looks at him. "Yes. Yes, I am," he answers.

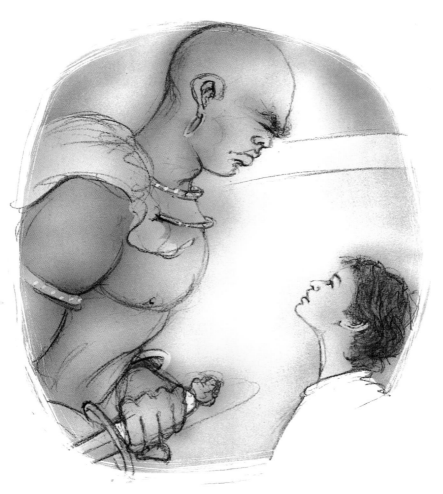

"Come with me," says the guard. "Queen Cleopatra likes your work. She wants to give you a job at the palace."

"But I *have* a job," Hapu says. "I work with my father. I can't leave him. You don't underst . . ."

"No. *You* don't understand," the guard says. "When the Queen gives you a job, you take it." He puts one hand on his sword. "Now go and say goodbye to your father."

At the palace Cleopatra talks to Hapu. She is wearing his necklace. "I want you to live here and make lots of beautiful things for me," she says.

"Thank you, Queen of the Nile," Hapu says. "But . . ."

"*But*?" The Queen looks at Hapu.

"But . . . I can't live here. You see, my father is very ill and . . ." Hapu tells the Queen everything.

At the end of Hapu's story, Cleopatra looks at him.
"All right," she says. "You can go home to your father.
But . . ." "But?" asks Hapu. "But from today, the two of
you work only for me. Do you understand?"
"Oh yes!" Hapu smiles. He is very happy. Now he and
his father can make lots of beautiful things and be rich.
"Yes, I understand."

ACTIVITIES

Pages 1–7

Before you read

1 Read the Word List at the back of the book. What are the twenty words in your language? Find them in a dictionary.

2 Look at the pictures in the book. What do you think?

    a Does Hapu work with his mother or his father?

    b Who is ill?

    c What does Hapu make for Queen Cleopatra?

    d Can he meet the Queen easily?

While you read

3 Finish the sentences.

    a "Bak" is the name of Hapu's ....

    b They make gold .... and chairs.

    c They aren't rich; they're ....

    d Bak is .... for two weeks.

    e Hapu makes a beautiful .... necklace.

    f He goes to Cleopatra's ....

    g "What do you want?" a palace .... asks.

    h Later, Hapu hears two men talking in the ....

After you read

4 Why …

    a is Bak ill?

    b do the guards at the palace stop Hapu?

    c is he happy about the market tomorrow?

Pages 8–15

Before you read

5 Look at the pictures. What do you think?

    a What does Hapu say to the Queen in the market?

    b Why does a guard come to Hapu's house?

While you read

6 What is first? What is after that? Write the numbers 1–8.

    a Cleopatra says, "You can go home to your father."   .....

    b One of the palace guards says, "Are you Hapu?"   .....

    c At the palace, Cleopatra talks to Hapu.   .....

    d Cleopatra looks at Hapu's necklace.   .....

    e Hapu says, "I can't live here".   .....

    f Cleopatra says, "Give this boy some money".   .....

    g The guard says, "Come with me".   .....

    h Bak sees the money from Cleopatra and is very happy.   .....

After you read

7 Look at the people in the pictures. What are they thinking?

    a the women in the street on page 9

    b Cleopatra on page 10

    c Bak on page 11

8 One of the guards tells a friend about Hapu. Write the guard's story. Start: *One day a poor boy comes to the palace.*

9 "The Fireboy" is a story from Ancient Egypt. What do you know about Egypt now? Write some sentences about Egypt.

WORD LIST *with example sentences*

Ancient (adj) This building is *ancient*. It is 2,000 years old.

end (n) Walk to the *end* of the road and go left.

factory (n) We make 100 cars every day in this *factory*.

fire (n) I'm cold. Let's sit near the *fire*.

gold (adj) This *gold* pen is $900.

guard (n) "Stop!" the guard says. "You can't come in here."

hard (adj/adv) The work is *hard*, but he is strong.

leave (v) People usually *leave* school at 17 or 18.

market (n) You can buy food in the shops or in the *market*.

necklace (n) The boy in this book makes a *necklace* for Cleopatra.

need (v) We *need* some food. Let's go to the shop.

palace (n) Queen Cleopatra lives in a big beautiful *palace*.

pay (v) They haven't got much money. They can't *pay* for a doctor.

poor (adj) They haven't got much money. They are *poor*.

Queen (n) *Queen* Elizabeth is the *queen* of England.

rich (adj) She has money, cars and houses. She is *rich*.

sword (n) The guards have long *swords*.

tell (v) He *tells* stories well.

tired (adj) I'm very *tired* but I can't sleep.

wear (v) She's *wearing* a black hat and a white shirt.

Pearson Education Limited
Edinburgh Gate, Harlow,
Essex CM20 2JE, England
and Associated Companies throughout the world.

ISBN: 978-1-4058-6957-7

First published 1991
New edition first published 1998
This edition first published 2008

10

Copyright © Longman Group Ltd 1991
This edition copyright © Pearson Education Ltd 2008
Illustrations by Chris Burke

Typeset by Graphicraft Ltd, Hong Kong
Set in 12/20pt Life Roman
Printed in China
SWTC/10

Published by Pearson Education Ltd

Every effort has been made to trace the copyright holders and we apologise in advance for any
unintentional omissions. We would be pleased to insert the appropriate acknowledgement in any
subsequent edition of this publication.

For a complete list of the titles available in the Pearson English Readers series, please
visit www.pearsonenglishreaders.com. Alternatively, write to your local Pearson Education
office or to Pearson English Readers Marketing Department, Pearson Education,
Edinburgh Gate, Harlow, Essex CM20 2JE, England.